THE WAY OF THE SOUL®
The Path To Self Empowerment

Author Ross Bonacci ©
Artist Heidi Meuwissen©
Registered® The Way Of The Soul 2010 All Rights Reserved
www.thewayofthesoul.com

YOU ARE BEAUTIFUL

Author Ross Bonacci ©   Artist Heidi Meuwissen ©

YOU ARE BEAUTIFUL

Copyright © 2011 Ross Bonacci and Heidi Meuwissen

All rights reserved. No part of this book may be used or reproduced by any means, graphic, electronic, or mechanical, including photocopying, recording, taping or by any information storage retrieval system without the written permission of the publisher except in the case of brief quotations embodied in critical articles and reviews.

Balboa Press books may be ordered through booksellers or by contacting:

Balboa Press
A Division of Hay House
1663 Liberty Drive
Bloomington, IN 47403
www.balboapress.com
1-(877) 407-4847

Because of the dynamic nature of the Internet, any Web addresses or links contained in this book may have changed since publication and may no longer be valid. The views expressed in this work are solely those of the author and do not necessarily reflect the views of the publisher, and the publisher hereby disclaims any responsibility for them.

ISBN: 978-1-4525-3199-1 (sc)

Library of Congress Control Number: 2010919536

Any people depicted in stock imagery provided by Thinkstock are models, and such images are being used for illustrative purposes only. Certain stock imagery © Thinkstock.

Printed in the United States of America

Balboa Press rev. date: 1/26/2011

YOU ARE BEAUTIFUL

You Are Beautiful is a series of insightful, thought provoking messages that promise to make you look deep inside, to find inspiration and help you reach your goals. Each of the 42 messages is inspired by one word.. The messages are written in conjunction with original artwork that ignites the truth behind them. The wonderful artwork will accentuate your experience of the allegories, mantras and positive statements in the messages.

Each message ends with a sacred intention. The intentions are meant to focus your capability to consciously reach your inner truth.

Use these messages as catalysts for changing your mood during a bad day, or to energize yourself before an important task. The words will each activate positive energy in you. The more you read, the more you will find your perspective becoming clearer, and your life changing for the better.

Thank you

From the bottom of my heart I thank you for purchasing

You Are Beautiful

It is a gift from me to you. I hope you will enjoy reading it as much as I have enjoyed writing it. I have poured my life's learning into this one book. I believe it will help you in many ways that words cannot describe.

It has been my absolute privilege and pleasure to give this book to you. The pages of this book carry the essence of life itself. That is yours to savour now...

Acknowledgment

I would like to thank my children Jaymes and Catherine who are the joy of my life and to Lorin Daher, Yasha Firooz and Ali Inayat for their loving guidance and creative inspiration.

A very special thank you goes to Heidi Meuwissen, a young artist who is truly amazing. She is gifted beyond her years, and was guided to me by God. Her art work is timeless, as it captures the very meaning of life within its frame.

- Ross Bonacci founder/Author of The Way of the Soul

ROSS BONACCI / FOUNDER

THE WAY OF THE SOUL – about the author

Ross Bonacci has studied and explored numerous healing modalities and is a Master of Reiki, Zenith Omega, and Avatar. He has been on the path of self discovery since his late teens and his great appreciation for life has inspired an enquiry into the human potential. He confesses that his soul guided him on his travels.

His journey has taken him too many sacred places both within himself and also geographical locations around the world. He embraces a multi denominational view point on the Cosmos and all that is.

The Way of the Soul is the distillation of his many trainings and his experiential understanding of them. Ross now; humbly, yet proudly presents to you his offering of thanks to all those who have been part of his Evolution;

You Are Beautiful is his gift to you to honour and accelerate your journey home to yourself.

May this book guide you home with ease and grace.

Ross resides in Sydney Australia. He is available for public lectures and teachings.

Heidi Meuwissen - About the Artist

Heidi Meuwissen has been painting since her early teens. Heidi's love for art has grown stronger and stronger year by year. She is passionate about color and bringing the healing power of art to life with her unique style.
Born 11th September 1989 and raised in Sydney Australia with a Dutch background, she attended Meriden Anglican School and went on to further her studies in art at National Art School in Darlinghurst Sydney [2008]

Heidi Achievements

Awards –
2010 - Liverpool art prize exhibition;
2009 - Selected Urban chalk pavement festival artist;
2007 - Senior lavender art and design prize.

Exhibition Groups

Liverpool Art Prize Exhibition, Chalk Pavement Exhibition, HSC Art Exhibition;

Heidi's art comes from the heart. She has a very beautiful open loving heart and is able to express her emotions though the journey of her art.
At the age of 21years she is truly an amazing gifted artist beyond her years.
Her artwork captures the meaning of life in its frame.

For more of Heidi's work visit her website at: www.heidimeuwissen.com
You are Beautiful introduces the following sacred symbolic
piece of art, intended to impart a sense of love, joy
and tranquillity into the heart of the reader.

HOPE

Hope shows you the way.

Hope is like a shining light when all you see is darkness. It is a profound and mysterious force that offers the possibility to transcend any seemingly impossible situation. In this lies its power.

Never give up on yourself. There is always hope. It is like a candle that burns through the rain. Hope will carry you to where you are meant to be.

Intention:
I am guided by the light of hope.

HOPE

I am guided by the light of hope.

HONOUR

Honour yourself.

Honour your role in this world. Honour the gifts that you have been given. Honour yourself by aligning yourself with your values.

Be humble and accepting of the life you have chosen for yourself.

Show honour and respect for the life of others too. Honour those around you by accepting the life they have chosen for themselves.

Once you respect yourself and others is when you are truly honourable.

Intention:
I honour myself

HONOUR

I honour myself

HONESTY

Be honest with yourself.

Honestly sets you free. Like King Arthur's sword, it is pure. It cuts through guilt, regret and all those human vices that hide our true selves.

Be honest with yourself, be honest with others.
Live an honest life, be an honest person.

The warrior carries a sword, your sword is honesty. It will protect you against intrigue, jealousy and envy. Be honest with yourself this is one of the greatest gifts you can give yourself.

Intention:
I am honest with myself

HONESTY

I am honest with myself

BELIEVE

Sometimes we feel lost in our lives, lost within ourselves.

Ahoy! To you, oh wise one; believe in thyself, for you have it all within you.

You are the one you have been looking for; you are the one you have been searching for.
You are the one you are praying for! You are the one you are praying to! Trust in yourself and know that you are there to be remembered. You are the one you seek. Remembering this, it is everything.

Intention:
I believe in myself

BELIEVE

I believe in myself

FAITH

Have faith in yourself.

When all you see is darkness, confusion, pain and worry, have faith, have faith, this will pass. Faith is like the stars, you might not see them through the storm, but they are always there, their light might be minute, but it is light. Like the stars, faith will guide you in.

Faith says to you," Do not worry; you are on the right path. You are just unable to see it at present, but you will."

Have faith in yourself for it opens up new paths for you, helps you weather the storms in your life, and remember, with faith, you will succeed.

Intention:
I have faith in myself.

I have faith in myself.

STRENGTH

Awaken your inner strength

Awaken the real you. Say this aloud in front of your mirror, and you will feel your spirit gathering your inner strength around you:

The strength of God is within me. I can see Archangel Michael standing before me, looking into my eyes as I ask for inner strength. I already have it within me. It is time to awaken from my deep slumber. It is time to reclaim my strength. I have the courage of a lion roaring through my veins, the strength of thousand men in me. I have the courage to be honest with myself and lovingly speak the truth. I am now strong.

Intention:
My truth gives me strength.

STRENGTH

My truth gives me strength.

MANIFESTATION

It is time to manifest.

Everything you have ever wanted has manifested. Be very clear with yourself about what it is that you wish to create in your physical universe.

Send your request to the divine and enclose a self-addressed envelope with it, so the divine can send it back to you.

Manifestation is a knowing of what is to be. Know that it will be. Just know it, feel it and you will be the person who has it.

Intention:
I am connected to my inner knowing.

MANIFESTATION

I am connected to my inner knowing.

MESSAGES

Be open to receiving messages from anyone,
anywhere, anyhow, at anytime.

You are continuously receiving messages but don't realise it.
Messages can be in any form. Be open to them. Look for them
in the elements, taking time to feel their message. The wind, the
rain, the sun and the moon can all be wonderful messengers.

Your dreams too, can be powerful messengers.
People are also messengers.
Even in sitting on a bus and overhearing a conversation the
Universe can be conveying what you need to hear.

Just stop and listen, you will start experiencing the
messages you need to help you move forward.

Intention:
I rest in my stillness

TRUST

I trust in me.

FORGIVENESS

Forgive yourself.

Remember your decisions in life were made because they were meant to be made. See your past as a time of growth. You must learn to accept.

Forgive yourself, forgive others, and move on. What you feel for yourself is reflected to you by others. Forgiving yourself is the first step on the path to healing. It will unlock your heart and give you access to the unlimited supply of kindness you have to share with all who cross your path.

Remember, forgiveness is a blessing from the self to the self.

Intention:
I love and forgive my self

FORGIVENESS

I love and forgive my self

WISH

Make a wish upon a star.

Look up into the heavens at night and see all the stars as they surround you like a blanket. The universe is so vast yet so warm.

Take a moment to be with the stars in the night sky. Expand into the vastness of the universe. Realise that all that you see outside of you is also within you.

Each of those stars is a wish waiting to come true. You just have to ask for it. It's the perfect time to make a wish. This is a time in your life when wishes do come true; the heavenly part of you grants them to you. Make a wish now. It will come true.

Intention:
My wish comes true

WISH

My wish comes true

OPPORTUNITY

Your moment is out there

Everyone has their time; your magical time will come soon. There will be a time in your life when you are at the right place at the right time. Your turn will come. Serendipity will show its face.

Remember, there are hundreds of possibilities right now. One of them is yours. You will embrace it.

When it comes, it will fill you with an indescribable completeness. You must at that time, humbly receive the grace of having your prayers answered.

Intention:
I embrace the opportunities that come my way

OPPORTUNITY

I embrace the opportunities that come my way

MUSIC

Dance and sing to the rhythm of life.

There is music in your heart and soul. Express it in your
life through every word, movement and gesture.

Music and song have the power to awaken unfelt feelings
and unsaid words in you. Let them resonate deep inside
you. You will feel them transport you beyond yourself.

Let music and song awaken parts of you that
you never knew existed before.

Intention:
My body moves to the music of life.

MUSIC

My body moves to the music of life.

THE ELDERS

We are always with you

The beloved elders are the holy men and women of days gone by, who once walked this planet as you do today. Imagine that they gather around you now. They honour the path of your soul on its earthly journey and help you recover your personal power.

Release into the golden flame all that no longer serves you and experience your inner light anew. There are always new beginnings; remember that whatever happens today, wherever life takes you, tomorrow is a new day. Your life is a reflection of whatever is in your mind, so think happy thoughts.

Know this my dear child that the elder's eternal presence is always with you.

Intention:
I humbly receive the guidance of those who have gone before me.

THE ELDERS

I humbly receive the guidance of those who have gone before me.

SEER

You have the abilities of the seer.

The seer is a servant of mankind who sees all; past, present, and future. The seer has the ability to see beyond this world. Their vision is multidimensional. They recognise life for its many illusions.

You too can achieve great success by being a 'seer' in your daily life. Imagine yourself as a seer. Listen to your true intuition. It is all within you. You'll know what to do, your inner self is pointing at it.

Use this, and you will achieve what your destiny is.

Intention:
I trust my inner vision.

SEER

I trust my inner vision.

TRAVEL

It is time to travel, the adventure begins.

Know that you must travel to discover your true essence.
Your soul has always been travelling. It has travelled through
many times, and places before you were born.

You must also travel in this life. Go from city to city, town to town,
and mountain to mountain. Discover the world and its people.
Only when you go outside will you gain on the inside.

As you travel, you will satiate your soul, gaining experience
and wisdom. Your curiosity beckons you. You discover new
experiences, make new friends, and reconnect with old ones.
You now bring out your inner traveller. Know that you will touch others
and leave your mark as you go through your great adventure.

Intention:
My life is a wondrous adventure

TRAVEL

My life is a wondrous adventure

UNITY

I embrace the power in unity.

You are never a mountain alone. But united
with many you are each a mountain.

Your soul-mates, your friends, your family, and your
acquaintances can all be part of your union. Synergise with
them, they are your strength, and your greatest assets.

Like the bees in a bee-hive, if you are together you are both a
formidable friend, and foe. You must create your own hive. Everyone has
a role to play. Together you are an unstoppable force. Create this union,
be its architect and you shall see that life will become easier for you.

Know that living in union will make you strong.

Intention:
I embrace the union.

UNITY

I embrace the union.

FRIENDSHIPS

Treasure the friendships you have in your life.

Some friendships come and go while others are with you always. In true friendship the connection is timeless. With them, no matter how much time has passed since your last meeting, you are still totally connected in this moment. It is as if it was just yesterday when you were last together.

Give thanks, as these friendships are very special. Your friends are always there for you. Honour their friendship. Connect with them again, and with all the love in your heart, cherish and thank your friends for being in your life.

Intention:
I love and appreciate my friends

FRIENDSHIPS

I love and appreciate my friends

HEART

Open your heart.

Fully experience your life through your heart, for it holds the key to fulfilment. Allow your physical heart to merge with your spiritual heart. Your heart centre is expanding now.

You have a much greater capacity to love than you've ever had in the past. The love you have in your heart fills the ocean many times over. The love of the entire Universe flows through you. Let it merge and blend with the hearts of all you meet.

Only when you are open is when you really experience, and live to your fullest potential.

Intention:
My heart is open.

HEART

My heart is open.

INNER PEACE

This is the time for reflection.

At times it feels like you are carrying the weight
of the world on your shoulders.

It only seems heavy in the absence of internal tranquillity.
Attain this now, take a long slow breath in, and as you exhale
release the worries of the world. Let your mind be still, let go of
the voices in your head and focus on balance in your life.

As you release your worries, you are beginning to feel peace
and balance in your own life. You feel you are at internal
peace. This causes a ripple effect that touches everyone around
you. The world around you comes into that alignment.
Your inner peace creates World peace

Intention:
I am at peace with myself and the world is at peace with me

INNER PEACE

I am at peace with myself and the world is at peace with me

FUTURE

Your future is your true north.

The future is where you will be. It is an open canvas where you can paint whatever you wish. Allow yourself to dream. Release your imagination. Your dreams will guide you to the future you want. Self-limiting thoughts are now removed from your consciousness.

It is time to live your future. You are your own compass; you are free from self limitation. You create your own future from the dreams you hold dear to your heart. Act in the present; live in the future, your future.

Intention:
My life is a, dream come true

FUTURE

My life is a, dream come true

FAMILY

Family is very important to you.

You have your biological family and you have your soul family. Your biological family is the family that you were born into. You chose to be born into your birth family to fulfil many past agreements.

You also have a soul family who connect with you at a deeper level. Realise that your soul family is gathering around you at this time. Gain from their synergies, they have come into your life to be with you, to support you, to guide you and to help you grow spiritually.

Connect with them, be with them. Learn to accept their help in times of need. Lean on them and with their support open up, and succeed.

Intention:
I enjoy wholesome loving connections with people

CHILDREN

I honour the child within

MYSTERIES

Discover the mysteries that you have within yourself.

There are many mysteries in life. There is much that is unknown to you. Embrace the unknown. Cherish it, for it causes you grow.

The mysteries are linked to time. They only reveal themselves when their time comes. You must allow them to unfold.

Let go of your fear and step into the unknown. Move into it with passion and excitement. They will carry you forward and help you embrace and then master each moment anew.
Be brave, take heart and just do it.

Intention:
I embrace the unknown

MYSTERIES

I embrace the unknown

TRANSFORMATION

Know that with each ending a new beginning is emerging.

Death is a transformation of who you were, into who you will become. It is the end of one cycle and the beginning of another one. It is a reminder to recognise the power of time.

Recognize that there are many little deaths and an equal number of rebirths every day. All things have a beginning and an end; relationships, friendships, work. When you run a race, isn't the finishing line the same as the starting line? Whether it is a physical death, or the end of a cycle of your life, take heart, move forward with vigour, make your transformation positive.

Intention:
I lovingly accept and integrate change in all areas of my life

TRANSFORMATION

I lovingly accept and integrate change in all areas of my life

EARTH

Honour the earth; cherish the earth, for it is your home.

Connect with the ground you walk upon, the earth fairies will show you the way. You can sense their presence everywhere. In the trees, in the flowers, the streams, the rocks and rivers, they are always there, working away. They nurture, and caress sincerely and with devotion.

You too need to care for and nurture Mother Earth; it is your home too. Always remember, your help is essential for the earth fairies. Your time to become more actively involved has come. Maybe you can join a tree planting group, conserve water, or begin recycling. As you help the earth, you will recognise that the earth also helps you in many ways. It is time to honour your only real sanctuary, your earth.

Intention:
I honour Mother Nature

EARTH

I honour Mother Nature

ABUNDANCE

Abundance is all around you, the flood gates
are open, and you have it all.

Abundance of love, of joy, of happiness, abundance of money,
abundance of loving relationships, abundance is flowing in
all areas of your life. Discover the treasures that are within
you. Realize that you have the ability to create abundance
beyond your wildest dreams in all areas of your life.

It all comes together for you now. It is reflected in all areas of your life.
Feel the Grace of the Universe showering upon you in every moment

Intention:
I celebrate the abundance in my life.

ABUNDANCE

I celebrate the abundance in my life.

ANGELS

The Angels are watching over you.

They are beautiful beings of light, who give you guidance from beyond. They are ready and willing to assist you at any time; Surrender your worries and concerns to them. These beautiful light workers bring you messages of love and light. They can assist you in any area of your life.

Call upon the Angels whenever you feel the need. Receive their loving guidance. Feel their love now. Imagine you are being bathed in the light of their love. The Angels are always there for you.

Intention:
I humbly ask and gratefully receive the help
of the angels in all areas of my life.

ANGELS

I humbly ask and gratefully receive the help
of the angels in all areas of my life.

BOUNDARIES

You are safe

You are a fortress within yourself. The walls of your fortress are of your own making. They are your circles of energy. Realise that your circles of energy are your deterrent as well as your gates for those around you.

If you feel unsafe, or unsure of yourself know that your energy is low. Only you can choose to bring it back up.

Focus on your energy, and you will create boundaries. They will assert your presence. They will be both welcoming for well wishers, and thwarting of those who can do you harm. You can feel them protecting you as your energy grows.

Intention:
I create my safety

BOUNDARIES

I create my safety

LOVE

Love yourself.

The love that you have inside your heart is an eternal presence. Learn to love who you are. Love is for the soul what the breath is for the body.

Open the door to your heart and allow
universal love to flow through you.
See and feel that love nourishing you and all those you meet.
Let your love enable you to feel the wind, the rain; the sound of
birds in the trees, and the fragrance of the flowers in the fields.

Look inside yourself and see yourself as a loving
being. When you recognize yourself as a loving being,
you see everyone and everything as love.

Intention:
I am love

LOVE

I am love

ANIMALS

Look listen learn
I am speaking to you

Animals appear to us in both spiritual and physical form. Our love for animals is so deep and dear. It is time to realise we have so much to learn from them. They teach us so many wonderful things about ourselves. They teach us to love unconditionally. They give us guidance.

Spend time listening to the animals around you. Take your dog for a walk. He speaks to you of friendship. Listen to the birds in the trees, they sing their songs of joy. Take notice of all the different animals that cross your path.

Be aware where your mind goes when you see them. This can be a special message just for you.

Intention: I recognise the Great Spirit in all beings

ANIMALS

I recognise the Great Spirit in all beings

JOY

Your joy touches people very deeply.

Smile, laugh, have fun, celebrate. Do what makes you truly joyous.
This is the time for you to discover what makes your
heart sing. Live with the innocence of a child.

Know that your joy and laughter are contagious. Your
joy touches people in a beautifully profound way, its
gives them hope. Let the gift of your joy touch the lives of
others. Be happy and joyous for no good reason.

Remember, only you can make it so that your
life is filled with joy and happiness.

Intention:
I choose to bring joy to all areas of my life

I choose to bring joy to all areas of my life

LEADERSHIP

Awaken the leader within you.

Each of us has a leader in us. We are all capable of being
the many things a leader is. We have all been resolute,
decisive and passionate in different times. We have also
been composed, humble and steadfast at times.

Realising that you are capable is the first step to leadership.
There are many master leaders that came before you.
Jesus, Buddha, Alexander the Great, Martin Luther King
and others; you have all of them and more in you.

Like a true leader, allow your innate sense of leadership to guide others
and yourself gracefully through life. Struggle, worry and fear disappear
from your consciousness; you are now centred in your persona.

Intention:
I am tomorrow's leader

LEADERSHIP

I am tomorrow's leader

SOUL-MATES

Your soul mate enters your life.

Everything around you is in pairs. Everything is born with a companion. Your companion is out there too. Some of you have found them, some will soon find them.

Understand that true love always finds a way of bringing two people together. Your life partner is yours forever. You will feel them when you come across them.

Once you find them, know that they are yours and yours only. You are deeply connected to them. Your spirits are one.

The moments you will share with your soul-mate are forever.

Intention:
I am in love

SOUL-MATES

I am in love

DOORWAYS

All I see is open doors.

Your soul has chosen to go through many doorways in its earthly incarnation. You see the doors to the past, they have now closed.

Doorways to the birth of something new are now visible, new stages in your life are now opening to you. This is truly an amazing time for you as an individual. New opportunities present themselves to you, one after the other. Choose from them with confidence.

You have been preparing for this your entire life. This is your time. Walk forward and fulfil your destiny.

Intention:
I fulfil my destiny

DOORWAYS

I fulfil my destiny

LIFE

Make something of your life, be the best you can be.

Life is a gift, cherish it, and honour it through
living in integrity with your highest truth.

You are continuously changing. With every outgoing breath you are releasing the person you were a moment ago. With every incoming breath you are expanding into your ultimate potential.

Renewing that possibility in every moment; every new experience you have helps shape who you are to become. You are not a stagnant being but a continuous unfolding of the gift of life. Move with the winds of change like a palm tree dancing in the summer breeze.

Intention:
I joyously surrender to the flow of life

LIFE

I joyously surrender to the flow of life

THE HIGHER BEINGS

Be one with those above you.

Realise that there is more out there than you are aware of. As gifted as we are, we realise we still have a long way to go to reach true enlightenment.

There will always be a higher existence, perhaps there exist whole civilizations. These high beings interact with you, helping you evolve into a higher state of being. They have been there through every age, bringing the language of light to mankind.

Integrate with them; use them to reach a higher state of conscious. You can feel you're physical and spiritual becoming one with their help. You are integrating with your higher self and becoming one with all things.

Intention:
I am one with all things

THE HIGHER BEINGS

I am one with all things

HEALING

You can heal your body.

Know that your existence is independent of your body. You don't live in your body, your body lives in you. It is merely a vehicle that you utilise.

If your body has pain or discomfort or is riddled with disease, realise that you have the ability to heal it. It is your existence; hence you have the power and ability to heal your body. Make peace with your illness, or your pain.

Imagine a ball of divine light igniting in the centre of your being. Your healing has begun. Take control of your body, you are in charge of your healing process.

Intention:
I am healed.

HEALING

I am healed.

PRAYER

It is time to pray

Prayer is the amalgamation of all the lessons from before. It releases you, and bounds you, you are both responsible, and carefree at the same time. Prayer is your servitude to the higher being, and acceptance of your limitations.

You honour yourself when you pray. Only a being of higher conscious can recognise the power that the higher being has manifested in you. You are special, gifted and your prayer is a confirmation of that.

So Pray, accept, recognise yourself and you will see the truth within you. As you pray you feel elated, refreshed, renewed. You also feel light, this is real freedom. Embrace it. Your prayer opens the vast and limitless love inside you.

Intention:
My life is an offering of love

PRAYER

My life is an offering of love

MIRACLES

Miracles are happening all around you.

Enjoy life for the many miracles it creates for you. All you need is to be aware and open. Follow the mantra below and you will see them!

I feel my consciousness is expanding. What a wondrous thing to witness. My awareness is rapidly increasing. I am now in an extended state of self-consciousness. My outside world is coming into alignment with my inside world. Everything in my life is reflecting my true self. I have now begun to realise my own power. My physical world is rapidly changing. I am an integral part of the miracle of life.

Intention:
I have the power to create miracles

MIRACLES

I have the power to create miracles

TRUTH

Follow your truth

Your truth is yours only. It lies deep within you. It is different from the truth that lies within others.

One must always follow one's own truth. What is your truth? Are you following it?

You can awaken your truth by trusting yourself. Ask your soul to reveal your truth to you and it will. Learn to follow the path that your soul has designed for you by trusting your instincts and following the signposts that life has laid out for you along the way.

You can only reach greatness by being one with the truth within you.

Intention:
I easily live my truth.

TRUTH

I easily live my truth.

KNOWLEDGE

It's time to gain a perspective
Knowledge is essential to your understanding of yourself. It enables you to make sense of the buzz of information all around you. Your knowledge is your lens, the more you have, the clearer you see life.

A deeper knowledge will assist you with any difficulties that you are having in your life. It will help you understand your circumstances.

However, know that knowledge never comes easily. You must appreciate its value for it to be revealed to you.

As you share and spread what you know, your knowledge will grow, and so will your appreciation for it.

Intention:
I appreciate knowledge

KNOWLEDGE

I appreciate knowledge

You have the power to create miracles

Ross Bonacci ©

YOU ARE BEAUTIFUL

Is Part Of
'The Way of the Soul'
Soul Card collection

THE END

Author Ross Bonacci ®
Artist Heidi Meuwissen®
www.thewayofthesoul.com
Registered® The Way Of The Soul 2010 All Rights Reserved